Drumpty Dumpty Had a Great Fall

"An Adult Nursery Rhyme Book"

Written by Jiminy Ricketts
Illustrated by Marcy Petricig Braasch

DrumptyDumptyBook.com

Copyrighted Material

Drumpty Dumpty Had a Great Fall
Copyright © 2021 by Natural State Design, LLC. All Rights Reserved.

No part of this publication may be reproduced, stored in a retrieval system or transmitted, in any form or by any means—electronic, mechanical, photocopying, recording or otherwise—without prior written permission from the publisher, except for the inclusion of brief quotations in a review.

For information about this title or to order additional books and/or electronic media, contact the publisher:

DrumptyDumptyBook.com
E-mail: info@DrumptyDumptyBook.com

ISBNs:
Print: 978-1-7371478-0-0
Kindle and ePub: 978-1-7371478-1-7

Printed in the United States of America

"This book is dedicated to Aunt Jill, whose idea it was for this project, and to all of the people, animals, and plants that this con man, posing as a president, harmed before, during, and after his presidency."

J.R.

Table of Contents

Don and Kell'..8
Rub-A-Dub-Pub..10
Trump Trump Tweet Away...............................12
My Brother Lies over the Ocean.......................14
I'm a Little Trump-pot.....................................16
The Donald and the Kell'.................................18
Raa, Raa, Republicans.....................................20
Where is Trumpkin..22
Drumpf Be a Prick...24
The Congress GOP Go Back and Forth...........26
We're Begging, Imploring...............................28
Twitter, Twitter, Little Trump.........................30
Hey 'Rona 'Rona...32
An Orange and Yellow Ass'ket......................34
Give it up Donnie...36
Drumpty Dumpty..38

Don and Kell'
To the tune of "Jack and Jill"

Don and Kell' went up The Hill
To pitch the wares of his daughter
Don fell down
Looking the clown,
And his cronies came fumbling after.

Rub-A-Dub-Pub
To the tune of "Rub-A-Dub-Dub"

Rub-a-dub-dub,
Three Trumps in a pub,
And who do you think they be?
The pusher, the taker, the real estate faker,
All smug as can be.

Trump Trump Tweet Away
To the tune of "Rain Rain Go Away"

Trump Trump tweet away,
We all know what you have to say.
Trump Trump tweet away,
Little Donnie wants his way.

My Brother Lies over the Ocean
To the tune of "My Bonnie Lies over the Ocean"

My brother lies over the ocean
My daughter lies over the sea
My family lies over the ocean
Trump, bring back my family to me...

I'm a Little Trump-pot
To the tune of "I'm a Little Teapot"

I'm a little Trump-pot,
Orange and stout,
Tryin' to get a handle
On what it's all about
When I watch my TV,
Hear me shout,
Take this news and throw it out!

The Donald and the Kell'
To the tune of "The Farmer in the Dell"

The Donald and the Kell'
The Donald and the Kell'
Oh no, here we go...
The world is headed to Hell

The Donald takes a life
The Donald takes a life
Oh no, a burial...
Someone take his knife

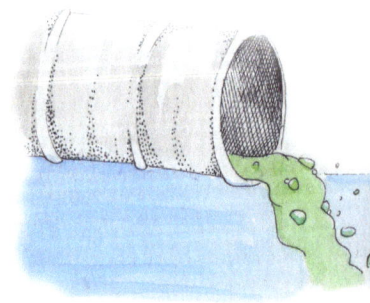

Raa, Raa, Republicans
To the tune of "Baa, Baa, Black Sheep"

Raa, raa, Republicans,
Have you any bull?
Yes, sir, yes, sir,
A Drumpster full!

Where is Trumpkin
To the tune of "Frère Jacques"

Where is Trumpkin?
Where is Trumpkin?
Tweeting live,
Tweeting live,
Get that phone away from him!
Get that phone away from him!
It's all lies.
It's all lies.

Drumpf Be a Prick
To the tune of "Jack Be Nimble"

Drumpf be racist,
Drumpf be a prick,
Drumpf thinks Corona
Is a dirty ol' trick.

The Congress GOP Go Back and Forth
To the tune of "The Wheels on the Bus"

The congress GOP go back and forth
Back and forth
Back and forth
The congress GOP get nothing done
All session long

We're Begging, Imploring
To the tune of "It's Raining, It's Pouring"

We're begging, imploring,
The old Trump's ignoring.
He's in his head and needs some meds,
'Cause he didn't wear a mask this morning.

Twitter, Twitter, Little Trump
To the tune of "Twinkle, Twinkle, Little Star"

Twitter, Twitter, little Trump,
Just to give your polls a bump.
Up above us all so high,
Like a demon in the sky.
Twitter, Twitter, little Trump,
You are just a fat orange grump!

Hey 'Rona 'Rona
To the tune of "Hey Diddle Diddle"

Hey 'rona 'rona!
It's been some time that Don has known ya,
He said you'd be gone in June;
The little doc cried
To see the report,
And we're still seeing in-laws over Zoom.

An Orange and Yellow Ass'ket
To the tune of "A-Tisket, A-Tasket"

A-tisket a-tasket
An orange and yellow ass'ket
A judge had stopped his Muslim ban
And now he's blown a gasket.

Give it up Donnie
To the tune of "Rock-a-bye Baby"

Give it up Donnie
Biden's on top.
When judges rule
Your lawsuits they'll stop.
When the news breaks,
The gavel will fall.
And down will come Donnie,
His ass they will haul.

Drumpty Dumpty
To the tune of "Humpty Dumpty"

Drumpty Dumpty sat on his wall,
Drumpty Dumpty had a great fall.
All of his sources and all of his kin
Couldn't put Drumpty together again.

THE END... of 4 years of hatred and regression by the Commander-in-Cheat.

www.ingramcontent.com/pod-product-compliance
Lightning Source LLC
Chambersburg PA
CBHW041705160426
43209CB00017B/1752